Derek Jeter

THE YANKEE KID

by
Jack O'Connell

SPORTS PUBLISHING INC.
www.SportsPublishingInc.com

©1999 Sports Publishing Inc.
All rights reserved.

Book design, editor: Susan M. McKinney
Cover design: Scot Muncaster
Photos: *The Associated Press; page 18, Columbus Clippers.*

ISBN: 1-58261-043-6
Library of Congress Catalog Card Number: 99-61950

SPORTS PUBLISHING INC.
SportsPublishingInc.com

Printed in the United States.

CONTENTS

After the Yankees' 1998 World Championship, Derek poured champagne on owner George Steinbrenner. (AP/Wide World Photos)

CHAPTER ONE

Becoming a Star

George Steinbrenner III, the principal owner of the New York Yankees, is no stranger to championships. In the 25 years he has run the Yankees, they have won six American League pennants and four World Series. He has made it clear over the years that even though he wants to win, when it comes to postchampionship celebrating, there shall be no spraying champagne on the owner.

In previous years, Steinbrenner was able to remain dry during such celebrations because players didn't want to risk making him mad. But after the Yankees won the World Series in 1998 to complete a record-setting season, Steinbrenner was drenched in the visitors clubhouse at San Diego's Qualcomm Stadium.

It wasn't difficult to find the person responsible. Derek Jeter, the fun-loving shortstop, crept up behind Steinbrenner while he was being interviewed on television and poured a bottle over his boss's head.

"Yeah, I know who did it," Steinbrenner said. "It was that Jeter kid. He knows he's not supposed to, but he did it anyway. And, you know, he's the only one I'd let get away with it. The way he has played for me, he can do whatever he wants.'"

Derek's relationship with Steinbrenner is similar to his relationship with almost everybody, playful and respectful. In his first three seasons in the major leagues, Derek Jeter has become one of the game's most popular players. Fans both young and old have quickly come to recognize and appreciate Derek's ability.

Derek has been an integral part of a Yankees renaissance in the 1990s. He was born less than an hour away from Yankee Stadium, grew up dreaming of playing for the Yankees and turned that dream into reality by starring on two World Series championship Yankees teams before his 25th birthday.

It will be difficult for the Yankees to improve upon their 1998 season. Including postseason play, the Yankees won 125 games and lost just 50. Their 114 regular-season victories established an American League record and were only two shy of the major-league mark set by the Chicago Cubs in 1906. The Yankees swept the Texas Rangers in three games in the Division Series, defeated the Cleveland Indians, four games to two, in the American League Championship Series and captured the

Derek has quickly become a star playing for the Yankees.
(AP/Wide World Photos)

World Series with a four-game sweep of the San Diego Padres.

As far as Derek is concerned, there is always room for improvement.

"There are still plenty of things I can do better" he said. "I could steal more bases. I could make fewer errors. I could strike out less. No one is perfect in baseball. A player can always do better."

That attitude has helped Derek stay on an even keel during his rise in the Yankees organization.

"Derek has a lot of exuberance, and it rubs off on the rest of our players," says Joe Torre, the Yankees' manager. "He has a lot of fun playing this game, and it shows. I've never been around anyone like him before. He's always upbeat, always looking at the positive side of things."

For the most part, Derek has handled himself professionally in the glass house of New York sports where reporters from eight daily newspapers and a

Derek enjoys watching the Knicks play at Madison Square Garden when he is in New York. (AP/Wide World Photos)

sports-talk radio station travel with the Yankees regularly, not to mention reporters from television stations and magazines who frequently visit Yankee Stadium.

Stardom in New York has been mostly positive for Derek, where reporters often want to know more about a player's life away from the ballpark than what he did during that day's game. Derek has tried to keep his personal life private, something other star New York athletes such as Mickey Mantle and Joe Namath struggled to do during their entire careers.

Says Yankees pitcher David Cone, "I've been with Derek at fan festivals and other personal appearances, and it's like being on tour with the Beatles. You'd think Derek was Ringo with all these girls screaming.... Derek has become one of those star athletes whose fame transcends sports."

Derek tries to keep his fame in perspective. He understands that his connection to the game and to the Yankees franchise plays an important part to his image.

"I want to represent baseball and the Yankees properly," Derek says. "Whatever I have is because of baseball. Whatever earning power I may have starts with the way I play baseball. One thing I've learned playing baseball is you can't take anything for granted. You can be on top one day and the next day it's a whole different deal. That's why my attitude has always been that I need to come to the park as prepared as I can be every day. You can't do that if you're out partying every night. I enjoy a good time, don't get me wrong, but I have plenty of time in the off-season for fun."

Derek has seen a lot of mistakes made by older players who became caught up in the celebrity lifestyle, and saw how it affected their performance on the field. He is determined not to let that happen to him.

He has signed some contracts for commercial endorsements, but he also turned down several opportunities. He has sought advice from teammates who have mellowed after making youthful mistakes earlier in their careers, such as David Cone, Darryl Strawberry and Dwight Gooden.

In their early days, Cone, Strawberry and Gooden were part of a Mets team in the 1980s that was as known for what it did away from the ballpark as it was for its fiery play on the field.

"There are plenty of examples to Derek in this room of what not to do," Cone said.

Added Strawberry, whose comeback was interrupted late in the 1998 season when he had to undergo surgery for colon cancer, "I realize I'm lucky to be alive. I look back and see all I did. It was crazy. I was young and didn't know how to handle it. I thought I was on top of the world and nothing could go wrong. It's an adrenaline rush to be recognized like that. It's hard to turn away from that kind of scene."

Strawberry has talked with Derek about not making the same mistakes.

"He comes from a good, solid family and has a strong value system," Strawberry said. "He knows that there are a lot of strangers out there who down deep don't really care for you. They just want to hang with somebody who's famous and make themselves feel important. Some people also get a kick out of dragging you down."

When Derek and Strawberry talk, it is often about the Turn 2 Foundation that Derek began in 1997 to create activities and programs designed to fight teenage substance abuse. It earned Derek the Joan Payson Award for community service from the

New York Chapter of the Baseball Writers' Association of America.

"As a kid, I was a big Dave Winfield fan," Derek said. "He had his Dave Winfield Foundation. I always said that if and when I ever made it I wanted to be like him and have my own foundation. I think everyone should give back. I'm not saying everyone should start a foundation, but I think everyone who's in this position should do something to help out."

Derek's regard for young people is also evident by the promise he made in 1997 to answer his fan mail on a daily basis. In the 85-minute interval after batting practice and before the start of the game, he can usually be found at a clubhouse table opening envelopes and signing photographs sent to him by his fans.

"My rookie year, I'd put it off for a week and I couldn't find my glove behind all the envelopes,"

Derek gets a hug from his father, Dr. Charles Jeter, after being named the American League Rookie of the Year in 1996. (AP/Wide World Photos)

Derek said. "Now I make a conscious effort to do it every day. Haven't missed one."

Derek credits his parents for his feet-on-the-ground attitude. His father, Dr. Charles Jeter, a drug and alcohol counselor, is an African-American, and his mother, Dorothy, an accountant, is an Irish-American. Derek has said he has been mistaken for Italian, French and Brazilian.

When he was named one of the 50 most beautiful people in the world by *People Magazine* in 1997, Jeter told the editors, "There's a mystery about me because people don't know what I am—black, white, Italian, Jewish. I can relate to a lot of people.

"Actually, I don't think of myself as black or white, but both," Derek said. "I can't feel another other way because it's all I know."

At a press conference at Yankee Stadium in 1994, young Derek Jeter was named Baseball America's minor league player of the year. (AP/Wide World Photos)

Born to Be a Yankee

Derek Sanderson Jeter was born June 26, 1974, in Pequannock, N.J., and remembers going to Yankee Stadium as a kid. While Derek was still in grade school, his family moved to Kalamazoo, Michigan. Although Derek's exposure to the major leagues was an occasional trip to Detroit's Tiger Stadium, the Yankees remained his favorite team. A poster of Dave Winfield hung on the wall of his bedroom.

Derek's dream was to play shortstop for the Yankees, and his play at Kalamazoo's Central High School drew the attention of scouts, including a former Yankees shortstop named Gene Michael, then the club's general manager. In his senior year, Derek batted .508 with four home runs and 23 RBI in 23 games and was named High School Player of the Year by the American Baseball Coaches Association.

"Everybody was telling me I'd get drafted in the first round," Derek said. "I didn't give the Yankees much thought, really, because everything I'd heard or read had me going to Cincinnati or Houston. When I heard the Yankees picked me, I was in heaven."

The Yankees had the sixth pick in the first round of the 1992 amateur draft and chose Derek, but there was talk in the organization that the 6-foot-3, 158-pounder would eventually be moved to third base.

"Our scouts at the time said that once Derek grew into his body, he might lose some agility and not be able to handle the shortstop position," said Michael, now a special scout for the Yankees. "He had a tough first year in the field, but we kept him at shortstop because it's easier to move a player off that position to another one. And, besides, there was no hurry."

Traditionally, the Yankees move players through their system slowly. Derek was aware of that and enrolled at the University of Michigan which he attended during the offseason after his first pro season, which he split between two Class A clubs, Tampa, Florida and Greensboro, North Carolina.

Derek played all of the 1993 season at Greensboro. While he did well offensively (.295, 71 RBI, 18 stolen bases), he committed 56 errors.

"High-error totals for a young shortstop aren't unusual," Michael said. "Shawon Dunston made over 70 errors one year in the minors, and he went on to become a very good major-league shortstop.

Derek spent the end of 1994 and the beginning of 1995 with the Triple A Columbus Clippers. (Tom Baldwin/ Columbus Clippers)

Derek was quick on his feet and was very coachable. I felt he'd make whatever adjustments were necessary."

Derek's breakthrough year was 1994. He played at three levels, batting .329 at Class A Tampa, .377 at Double A Albany, New York, and .349 at Triple A Columbus, Ohio. He was named Minor League Player of the Year by *Baseball America, The Sporting News, USA Today, Baseball Weekly* and Topps.

Still, the Yankees were not certain Derek was ready for the majors. They signed a free-agent shortstop, Tony Fernandez, to a two-year, $3-million contract to play full-time in 1995 and be an insurance policy if it turned out Derek was not ready to take over the job by 1996.

Derek was convinced he was ready.

Derek is known as a young man who manages to be both playful and respectful. (AP/Wide World Photos)

Ready for the Majors

Derek came to his first major-league training camp in the spring of 1995, the last year the Yankees trained at Fort Lauderdale, Florida, before they moved across the state to Tampa. Derek knew he had no chance to make the team, but he enjoyed the atmosphere and getting to be on the field with another of his heroes, first baseman Don Mattingly.

"Talk about weird, man," Derek said. "There I was, a 20-year-old kid on a field standing next to Wade Boggs and throwing the ball across the diamond to Don Mattingly. I couldn't believe it. One time, Donnie and I were coming off one of the back fields after doing our sprints and crossing the main field to get to the clubhouse. Nobody was around, not even the grounds crew. We were walking, then Donnie said we better run because you never know who's watching. I'll never forget that."

Derek opened that season at Columbus, but he got his chance to wear a Yankees uniform in late May. Fernandez was suffering from a strained right ribcage muscle and was placed on the 15-day disabled list. With second baseman Pat Kelly also hurt after being hit in the left wrist by a pitch, the Yankees needed help in the infield. They recalled Derek, who reported to the team and then-manager Buck Showalter May 29 in Seattle.

It marked the first time in 11 years a former No. 1 draft choice had reached the majors with the Yankees, since Rex Hudler played in nine games in

1984. To make roster space for Derek, the Yankees released veteran shortstop Kevin Elster, who was 2-for-17 (.118) that year and 2-for-37 (.054) in two seasons with the Yankees. Elster later made it back to the majors with the Texas Rangers. At 20, Derek was the youngest Yankee on the roster since pitcher Jose Rijo, who made the club out of spring training in 1984 at the age of 18.

"I hadn't thought much about being called up this year," Derek said. "I knew they weren't just going to give me the shortstop job. It's something you have to earn. I don't want anybody giving me a job. I want to win one. I'll try to keep doing the things I was doing down there [minors] at this level. It's still the same game. It's still baseball."

At Columbus, Derek was batting .354 with 18 RBI and eight stolen bases in 46 games, all at shortstop where he committed 12 errors. He was leading the International League in hits (62), doubles

*Derek makes one of his spectacular throws for a double play.
(AP/Wide World Photos)*

(13) and triples (5), ranked third in batting average and runs (32) and fourth in on-base average (.423) and extra-base hits (1 8).

Asked if he felt he had conquered the Triple A level, Derek said, "You can't conquer anything in baseball unless you hit 1.000 and don't make any errors. There's always a way you can improve your game. I still have to work every day to improve."

When Fernandez came off the disabled list June 8, the Yankees kept Derek and instead returned another infielder, Robert Eenhhorn, to Columbus. With Kelly still recovering from wrist surgery, the Yankees decided to have Fernandez play second base for the time being. The Yankees' double-play combination became the regular shortstop at second base and the heir apparent to his job.

"I probably made the best presentation to a player I've ever made," Showalter said. "You're dealing with a player who has an outstanding track

Derek has become an impressive defensive shortstop.
(AP/Wide World Photos)

record at his position and asking him to sacrifice that for the good of the team while a rookie plays his position. I don't want to offend him in any way. Tony was great about it. I said all along I wouldn't have Derek here unless he could play short every day. I don't want Derek playing second base here. He's not familiar with the position. I don't want a rookie having to deal with a position change in his first month in the major leagues."

Those plans didn't last long, due in part to the fact the Yankees were struggling at the time. They were in a stretch where they had lost 20 of 26 games and the club record was 16-25. Derek was hitting .234 with three doubles, one triple, six RBI and two errors. On June 12, the Yankees decided to send him back to Columbus, a big disappointment for Derek because the following day the Yankees were scheduled to play in Detroit. That would have given Derek his first chance to play in front of fans in his home state.

"I liked what I saw of Derek's bat speed and his range at shortstop," Showalter said. "He was not intimidated by this level of play at all. Part of his development was served well by his being here."

Fernandez moved back to shortstop, and Randy Velarde took over at second base. The moves worked well enough that the Yankees were in the race for the wild-card spot in the playoffs when they expanded the roster in September and brought Derek back to the majors.

The Yankees did make the playoffs, but lost a dramatic series to the Seattle Mariners, falling 6-5 in 11 innings in the fifth and deciding game.

As Derek and the team began preparing for the 1996 season, a big change occurred. Buck Showalter decided to leave the Yankees to become the leader of the expansion Arizona Diamondbacks. The Yankees in turn hired Joe Torre as their new manager.

As he left for Florida and the start of spring training, Derek didn't know what that change would mean for him.

As a minor-league prospect, Derek impressed Yankee coaches with his bat speed. (AP/Wide World Photos)

CHAPTER FOUR

Winning a Job

The first controversy of the Yankees' 1996 training camp occurred February 20, the first day the entire club assembled. Fernandez declared he would rather play someplace else because he suspected his shortstop job was being handed to Derek, which it probably was although no one would come out and say it.

"Derek Jeter hasn't won anything yet," said Bob Watson, then the general manager. "Tony Fernandez could be the everyday shortstop. You never know."

Nothing was in stone, naturally, but the Yankees' plans did call for Derek to get every possible chance to replace the 33-year-old Fernandez, who was considered a disappointment in 1995. Fernandez had hit .245—including only a .195 average righthanded—and had been erratic defensively.

Derek maintained the same attitude he had shown the day he was called up by the Yankees in 1995.

"It's not like I've been told I'm the shortstop no matter what," he said. "I have to prove I can handle the job. Nothing's worth having that you don't earn."

Said Fernandez, "As far as I know, there is no competition. The only thing I know is they want to go with him. That's what Joe told me over the winter."

Derek celebrates as he crosses the plate to score a game-winning run. (AP/Wide World Photos)

Torre claimed he misspoke in the off-season about the shortstop situation and modified his position in training camp by saying, "What I meant is that Jeter would get the opportunity to win the job. I read a newspaper story in which Jeter was quoted as saying he didn't want the job handed to him, that he wanted to earn it. The kid put it better than I did."

Regardless of the manner in which the information was relayed, Fernandez had only one interpretation—the Yankees preferred another shortstop over him.

"They want to go with a younger player." Fernandez said. "I have seen this happen before. I was on the other side at the time."

In 1984, Fernandez had replaced Alfredo Griffin as the Toronto Blue Jays' shortstop.

"Having been through this before, I understand what they're doing," Fernandez said. "It's business.

I think they have made up their minds. I know I can still play the game. If not here, then somewhere else. I don't want to cause trouble."

Fernandez went back to playing second base while Pat Kelly was recovering from right shoulder tendinitis. Then on March 24, Fernandez had real trouble. He fractured a bone in his right elbow while diving for a ground ball in an exhibition game. The injury required surgery, and Fernandez was lost for the entire season, which left the Yankees without a safety net for Derek.

Kelly's shoulder condition worsened, and the Yankees' second base job eventually went to Mariano Duncan, the veteran infielder who had been signed as a utility player. Rookie Andy Fox took over the backup role.

Late in camp, the Yankees' front office still wasn't convinced Derek was ready, and Watson made some phone calls looking for a veteran shortstop. Torre and his coaching staff felt Derek had shown enough in spring training to get the opportunity to play every day.

"I told Derek I didn't want him becoming overly concerned about his hitting," Torre said. "He had hit at every level, so I wasn't worried about that. I said if he hit .250, I'd be satisfied. But I needed him to concentrate on playing solid defense at shortstop. After that, he settled down and did a good job in the field. He started to hit, too."

Steinbrenner, always skeptical of rookies, had second thoughts about Derek, but he let Torre talk him out of going after another shortstop.

"I would not have gone with a Jeter in the past," Steinbrenner said. "I think I've changed. I was too demanding, too hasty. We know the ability is there. I've been looking for things to go wrong. Every year you look for him to stumble, but he doesn't stumble.

Derek receives contratulations from third base coach Willie Randolph after one of his career-high 19 home runs. (AP/Wide World Photos)

We force-fed him at three levels, and he dominated at each level. He could be one of those special ones."

Derek became the first rookie to open the season at shortstop for the Yankees since Tom Tresh in 1962. Derek hit his first major-league home run on Opening Day, April 2, at Cleveland's Jacobs Field, but not everything went smoothly as the season got underway. He rushed too many of his throws and made some careless errors and struggled to keep his batting average above .250. He found himself vulnerable to pitches on the outside corner of the plate. But he came to the park early every day and worked hard, which impressed the Yankees' coaches. Third base coach Willie Randolph, a former All-Star second baseman, took special interest in Derek.

"You never really know about a young player until you see how he handles adversity," Randolph said. "I told him not to peek at that pitch two inches off the plate because the umpire will ring him up.

A rookie has to swing at those pitches. Unlike a lot of young people today, Derek is very receptive to whatever you say. He also initiates conversations. He always wants to learn."

Randolph took Derek out to lunch at least once on every road trip. The coach hadn't forgotten how veterans such as Catfish Hunter, Lou Piniella and Chris Chambliss made him feel welcome as a rookie with the Yankees in 1976.

"I didn't lecture him," Randolph recalled. "It wasn't a 'Do this, don't do that' kind of thing. I wanted to help him feel comfortable. Derek told me over the winter how he longed for this opportunity, and he wanted to make the best of it."

Derek said, "I heard during spring training this job was mine to lose, but nobody told me that. Besides I consider that negative thinking. I just wanted the chance to win the job. I mean, there's no better job than being the shortstop for the New York Yankees. I've dreamed of it all my life."

Added Randolph, "Derek was open to constructive criticism. He can make the plays that get shown on ESPN, but I wanted him to concentrate on routine plays. Derek has a tendency to leave his feet too much, which probably comes from playing so many games on artificial turf at Columbus. He's now making better use of his range and arm, which are his assets."

In the dugout at Camden Yards one night, Randolph caught Derek observing Cal Ripken, then still playing shortstop for Baltimore.

"Cal knows hitters so well he's always in position." Randolph said. "He has a steady movement with each pitch. Derek's movements between pitches are kind of herky jerky. But he's young. A lot of this stuff comes with time. So far, so good, but let's give Derek some time."

Against the Orioles in the 1996 ALCS Derek hit a home run that became famous because a young fan interfered with the ball. (AP/Wide World Photos)

Derek batted .350 in the second half and finished the year with a .314 average, which made him the first New York shortstop in 40 years to hit .300 over a full season. Gil McDougald, the Yankees' first Rookie of the Year Award winner in 1951, hit .311 in 1956 when he replaced Phil Rizzuto at shortstop.

Derek's 183 hits were the most by a Yankee in 1996, and his 17-game hitting streak was the longest by a Yankees rookie since an 18-game streak by Joe DiMaggio in 1936. Derek drove in 78 runs, the highest RBI total for a rookie shortstop since the Cleveland Indians' Julio Franco had 80 in 1980. The total tied Frankie Crossetti (1936) for the second most RBI from a Yankees shortstop. Lynn Lary holds the club RBI record by a shortstop in one season with 107 in 1931.

The Yankees won the AL East title for the first time in 15 years. In 15 postseason games, Derek hit .361 with three doubles, one home run and three RBI. His home run was one of the biggest stories of the postseason, a game-tying shot in Game 1 of the ALCS at Yankee Stadium against the Orioles that was actually interfered with by a schoolboy fan.

After the Yankees defeated the Texas Rangers, three games to one, in the Division Series, they entered the ALCS against Baltimore, a team they had defeated 10 times in 13 games during the regular season. But Baltimore had a 4-3 lead in the eighth inning when Derek came to bat.

He already had three hits in the game, and the fourth would be the most talked about hit of that postseason. It was a fly ball that right fielder Tony Tarasco, who had entered the game for injured Bobby Bonilla, was set to catch on the warning track.

But 12-year-old Jeffrey Maier of Old Tappan, New Jersey, and his trusty glove intercepted the ball on its downward arc. The fan gloved the ball at the top of the wall. Tarasco pointed to the boy, but right field umpire Rich Garcia signaled home run. That brought Orioles manager Davey Johnson out of the dugout. Within seconds, Johnson and every Baltimore player in the field was standing in right field complaining to the umpires. Johnson's tirade grew heated enough for Garcia to eject him.

"I thought the ball was going out of the ballpark," Garcia said after the game. "I really didn't feel that Tarasco was going to catch the ball, so I called it a home run."

After seeing a videotape replay, Garcia said he probably should have called fan interference but not an out. "In retrospect, I might have put Jeter on second base," Garcia said.

''I don't know what happened." Derek said. "I had my head down and was running. I watched the

*Derek and pitcher John Wetteland (right) celebrate a win during the
1996 World Series. (AP/Wide World Photos)*

ball go toward the fence. But I wasn't sure if it was out, so I had to get on the move."

The Orioles played the game under protest, but since the play in question was a judgment call Baltimore had no legal retaliation. Garcia's call helped turn the direction of the game. It evened the score and gave the Yankees encouragement. They went on to win, 5-4, on a home run in the 11th inning by Bernie Williams.

The Orioles felt they had been robbed, which gave them something in common with Derek later on. Baltimore won Game 2 behind David Wells, who would become one of Derek's teammates in 1997, but the Yankees won the next three games in Baltimore to advance to the World Series against the Atlanta Braves.

On the workout day prior to Game 1 at Yankee Stadium, Derek walked out of his apartment on Manhattan's Upper East Side and discovered his

Alex Rodriguez, second from right, and Derek, center, are close friends as well as rivals. (AP/Wide World Photos)

car, a Mercury Mountaineer, had been stolen. It was the roughest period of the postseason for the Yankees, who lost the first two games of the Series at home before the Series moved to Atlanta for three games.

They didn't lose another game. Torre returned to the city where he had played and managed and emerged triumphant with three victories that sent the Series back to the Bronx, where the Yankees wrapped up the championship by beating Greg Maddux in Game 6. It was the 23rd championship in franchise history, but their first in 18 years.

Not surprisingly, Derek was a unanimous choice of the BBWAA as the American League winner of the Jackie Robinson Rookie of the Year Award.

"I had so many people ask me about this award the past few weeks, and I didn't know what to say," Derek said at the time. "I'm glad to hear it's official. This is great. The whole season was a great experience for me. You can't ask for more than to win the World Series in your first year. When you see someone like Joe Torre having waited so long [35 years] to get to the Series, you really appreciate it."

"You just can't overlook what Derek has done," Torre said. "To break in as a shortstop in New York City on a club that went to the World Series and be an important part of that success is really phenomenal. Derek has a maturity beyond his years."

Derek's season may have been overshadowed somewhat by the remarkable year of another young shortstop, Seattle's Alex Rodriguez, a close runnerup to Texas right fielder Juan Gonzalez for the American League Most Valuable Player Award. Despite being rivals on the field, Derek and Alex are close friends. Each stays in the other's apartment when the Yankees play the Mariners.

"I'm Alex's biggest fan." Derek says. "I brag on him so much that my teammates are sick of me talking about him."

Derek and Rodriguez are part of a new generation of talented shortstops that also includes Boston's Nomar Garciaparra, Cleveland's Omar Vizquel, Toronto's Alex Gonzalez, St. Louis' Edgar Renteria and the New York Mets' Rey Ordonez.

"This may be the best group ever to come up, certainly the best in a long time," Derek said. "The most important part of a shortstop's game is still the glove. If you can't hold down the position, then you can't play here, but now a lot of shortstops hit as well. I think guys like Cal Ripken, Alan Trammell and Barry Larkin changed the perception of shortstops. They were great hitters, so now a shortstop has to be able to hit to draw interest from scouts. I remember in the minors how shortstops seemed to work more on their hitting."

The success of his rookie season did present a problem for Derek. What would he do for an encore?

CHAPTER FIVE

Another Championship

Derek did not suffer from the so-called sophomore jinx in 1997, although his .291 average was 23 points below his 1996 average. Nevertheless, he had 190 hits, seven more than the previous year, and 48 extra-base hits, also seven more than his rookie year total.

He had the same number of home runs, 10, scored eight more runs at 116, but his 70 RBI were eight fewer than the year before. What bothered Derek most, however, was the Yankees' loss to the Indians in the Division Series.

Derek went to his first All-Star game in 1998. (AP/Wide World Photos)

"We felt we were the better team," Derek said. "That doesn't take anything away from the Indians. They beat us, fair and square, but it was tough watching someone else go to the World Series."

The Yankees certainly made up for that in 1998. From the first day of spring training, they were on a mission, but no one could have foreseen the kind of season they would have, especially when they opened the year by losing four of their first five games.

That poor start prompted a team meeting in Seattle in which the players essentially scolded each other for somehow losing the intensity level they developed in spring training. They went on an eight-game winning streak and maintained a torrid pace that brought them to the All-Star break with a 61-20 record, the best first-half record in history.

Derek was named to his first All-Star game, along with teammates David Wells, Paul O'Neill,

Derek sprays a teammate with champagne to celebrate the Yankees' 1998 American League Championship. (AP/Wide World Photos)

Scott Brosius and Mariano Rivera by Indians manager Mike Hargrove, who picked Derek over Garciaparra. Derek even challenged teammate Bernie Williams briefly for the AL batting title. His average peaked at .335 September 6, but he was still 12 points behind Williams, who held on to win at .339. Derek finished fifth at .324.

In addition to his batting average, Derek set career highs in home runs (19), RBI (84), hits (203), triples (8), stolen bases (30) and runs scored (a league-leading 127). In BBWAA balloting for MVP, Derek finished third behind winner Juan Gonzalez and runnerup Nomar Garciaparra.

His biggest satisfaction, however, came in helping the Yankees reclaim their title as World Champions, winning the American League pennant and then sweeping the Padres in the World Series. All of their 114 wins in the regular season would have been meaningless if the team had not gone on to win the World Series and nobody knew that better than Derek.

"Derek deserves the recognition," Torre said. "He makes everyone on our team better. He'll be our next team leader."

Derek defers that distinction now to the veterans on the team, such as O'Neill, Cone, first baseman Tino Martinez, and catcher Joe Girardi. Whether he admits it or not, Derek has definitely moved into that inner circle.

One drawback to being an attention getter is that pitchers often make such players targets. Derek is not an overly flashy player, but his high-profile image may give the appearance to some pitchers that he is strutting. He has been thrown at quite a bit, but he seldom retaliates.

One exception was June 24, 1997 in Detroit when Tigers righthander Doug Brocail hit Derek with a pitch above the left wrist after Chad Curtis had hit a two-run home run in the ninth inning of a come-from-behind Yankees victory. Derek exchanged words with the pitcher while going to first base.

"I didn't say anything to him until he said something to me," Derek said. "He told me to 'Get the ----- to first' and I said something back. I'm not going to charge the mound just because I get hit, but I'm not going to run, either."

The next day, Torre took Derek out of the lineup.

"What happened the previous game had nothing to do with it," Torre said. "I planned to give him this day off all along. I think all players need a rest now and then, although I know Derek doesn't agree with me. He wants to play every inning of every game."

Derek had started all 74 of the Yankees' previous games and had played in all but five of their

Derek stretches before the third game of the 1998 World Series.
(AP/Wide World Photos)

676 innings to that point. "At this rate, I'll never catch Cal Ripken," Derek said, smiling.

During his rookie season, Derek played in 108 straight games, a stretch that ended when Torre rested him in the second game of a September 25 doubleheader against Milwaukee at Yankee Stadium. The Yankees' victory in the first game clinched the AL East title.

"I tried to talk him out of it, but he insisted," Derek said. "My first game back I went 0-for-5 and the next day I was 0-for-4 with two errors, so I don't see how the rest helped. I just like playing. I hate watching. I like to play every day, but 14 years like Cal, I don't know. As long as Mr. Torre manages the Yankees I got no shot!"

Derek enjoys playing for Torre, but that doesn't mean he doesn't get under his skin once in a while. This almost always occurs when Derek is out of the lineup. In 1998, Derek had his first experience with

Derek has been very careful about maintaining a good public image.
(AP/Wide World Photos)

being placed on the disabled list because of a strained abdominal muscle. As reinstatement time neared, Derek drove Torre crazy on the bench.

"He can't stand being in the dugout," Torre said, "and what he does is sit right next to me and he doesn't shut up. No one will be happier when Derek is healthy again than I'll be."

Torre considers that a good type of complaining. Derek has never been one to complain or criticize. Part of his popularity comes from the care he gives to his image. It doesn't appear phony, either, but a genuine sense of courtesy and decency he learned at home.

"The thing that always impressed me about Derek was how receptive he was to coaching," said Stump Merrill, the former Yankees manager and long-time minor-league manager who had Derek in Columbus. "You could tell the first time you talked to him that he obviously came from a very good family. He's a very respectful person."

Derek's parents cautioned him about being careful what he said to the press, especially in New York, where a seemingly harmless quote can turn into a glaring headline.

"We wanted to make sure if he was talking to reporters that he was minding his P's and Q's," Dorothy Jeter told *The New York Times.* "It was not to put reporters down, but you heard so many horrible things about reporters and people in general. That's why we talked to Derek so much."

"I try not to pay attention to newspapers," Derek said. "I don't like hearing people who only talk about themselves."

Derek's closest friend on the Yankees when he broke in was Gerald Williams, an outfielder who now plays for Atlanta. Williams, a thoughtful and cordial man but somewhat suspicious of reporters, conveyed to Derek the value of not drawing too much attention to himself. Williams accurately anticipated what was in store for Derek if he fulfilled his potential.

"I've tried to be my own person, which isn't really that hard," Derek said. "I love playing baseball and having fun with the guys. I also know the things I have to do to get better."

Even in the winter, Derek can most often be found in the house he bought in Tampa in 1997 so he could be near the Yankees' minor-league complex. In early January, Derek has daily hitting sessions with Gary Denbo, the Yankees' minor-league batting instructor.

Derek wisely sensed that his .149 average against Seattle in 1997 would convince clubs to take the Mariners' approach against him, which is to pound him inside with fastballs. Derek had devel-

Derek, left, and Tim Raines wait their turn at batting practice. (AP/Wide World Photos)

oped an automatic inside-out swing at inside pitches and felt he needed to change that approach.

"I did some weight work to build up my upper body," Derek said. "I wanted to be able to turn on those pitches to be quicker inside, to drive those balls and not give up on them. Batting between Chuck Knoblauch and Paul O'Neill and with all the good hitters we have, I see a lot of fastballs."

The results have been there for Derek Jeter. As his mother says, "He's more than just a baseball player. He's Derek."

Derek rounds the bases after hitting a home run. (AP/Wide World Photos)

Derek Jeter Quick Facts

Full Name:	Derek Sanderson Jeter
Team:	New York Yankees
Hometown:	Pequannock, New Jersey
Position:	Shortstop
Jersey Number:	2
Bats:	Right
Throws:	Right
Height:	6-3
Weight:	195 pounds
Birthdate:	June 26, 1974

1998 Highlight: Finished third in American League MVP balloting.

Stats Spotlight: His .308 career batting average is among the top 12 active major league players.

Little-Known Fact: *People Magazine* selected Derek as one of the world's 50 most beautiful people in 1997.

Derek Jeter's Professional Career

Year	Club	AVG	G	AB	R	H	2B	3B	HR	RBI	BB	SO	SB
1992	Tampa	.202	47	173	19	35	10	0	3	25	19	36	2
	Greensboro	.243	11	37	4	9	0	0	1	4	7	16	0
1993	Greensboro	.295	128	515	85	152	14	11	5	71	58	95	18
1994	Tampa (FSL)	.329	69	292	61	96	13	8	0	39	23	30	28
	Albany	.377	34	122	17	46	7	2	2	13	15	16	12
	Columbus	.349	35	126	25	44	7	1	3	16	20	15	10
1995	Columbus	.317	123	486	96	154	27	9	2	45	61	56	20
	Yankees	.250	15	48	5	12	4	1	0	7	3	11	0
1996	Yankees	.314	157	582	104	183	25	6	10	78	48	102	14
1997	Yankees	.291	159	654	116	190	31	7	10	70	74	125	23
1998	Yankees	.324	149	626	127	203	25	8	19	84	57	119	30
Minor League Ttls		.306	447	1751	307	536	78	31	16	213	203	264	90
Yankees Totals		.308	480	1910	352	588	85	22	39	239	182	357	67
Post Season Ttls		.308	33	133	25	41	5	1	3	8	14	28	7

Career Fielding Statistics

Year	Team	Posn	G	GS	TC	PO	A	E	DP	FLD%
1995	Yankees	SS	15	14	53	17	34	2	7	.962
1996	Yankees	SS	157	156	710	244	444	22	83	.969
1997	Yankees	SS	159	159	719	244	457	18	87	.975
1998	Yankees	SS	148	148	625	223	393	9	82	.986
	Fielding Ttls		479	477	2107	728	1328	51	259	.976
Post Season Fldg Ttls			33	33	150	60	86	4	17	.973

A.L. Rookie of the Year Winners in the 1990s

1998	Ben Grieve
1997	Nomar Garciaparra
1996	**Derek Jeter**
1995	Marty Cordova
1994	Bob Hamelin
1993	Tim Salmon
1992	Pat Listach
1991	Chuck Knoblauch
1990	Sandy Alomar Jr.

Derek is 12th in career batting average among players who are still active. (AP/Wide World Photos)

Active Career Batting Average Leaders

1.	Tony Gwynn	.339
2.	Mike Piazza	.333
3.	Wade Boggs	.329
4.	Frank Thomas	.321
5.	Edgar Martinez	.318
6.	Alex Rodriguez	.313
7.	Kenny Lofton	.311
8.	Rusty Greer	.310
9.	Mark Grace	.310
10.	Nomar Garciaparra	.309
12.	**Derek Jeter**	**.308**

*Derek placed third in the 1998 American League MVP voting.
(AP/Wide World Photos)*

1998 AL MVP Voting

Player, Team	1st	2nd	3rd	Points
Juan Gonzalez, Texas	21	7	—	357
Nomar Garciaparra, Boston	5	7	7	232
Derek Jeter, New York	**2**	**6**	**1**	**180**
Mo Vaughn, Boston	—	3	1	135
Ken Griffey Jr., Seattle	—	—	4	135
Manny Ramirez, Cleveland	—	1	3	127
Bernie Williams, New York	—	1	3	103
Albert Belle, Chicago	—	—	4	96
Alex Rodriguez, Seattle	—	2	1	92

Game by Game with Derek Jeter in 1998

Following is a regular-season game-by-game breakdown of Derek Jeter's 1998 campaign in which he placed fifth among the American League batting leaders and third in the Most Valuable Player balloting.

Date	Opp	AB	R	H	2B	3B	HR	RBI
4/01/98	@Ana	4	0	0	0	0	0	0
4/02/98	@Ana	4	0	1	0	0	0	1
4/04/98	@Oak	3	1	1	0	0	0	1
4/05/98	@Oak	6	1	1	0	0	0	1
4/06/98	@Sea	3	0	0	0	0	0	0
4/07/98	@Sea	5	2	2	1	0	0	0
4/08/98	@Sea	5	1	1	1	0	0	0
4/10/98	OAK	5	1	0	0	0	0	0
4/11/98	OAK	5	2	2	1	0	0	0
4/12/98	OAK	5	1	1	0	0	0	0

Date	Opp	AB	R	H	2B	3B	HR	RBI
4/15/98	ANA	3	1	1	0	0	0	0
4/17/98	@Det	3	2	2	0	0	1	3
4/18/98	@Det	5	3	3	0	0	0	1
4/19/98	@Det	4	0	0	0	0	0	0
4/20/98	@Tor	6	0	1	0	0	0	0
4/21/98	@Tor	4	2	2	0	0	1	1
4/22/98	@Tor	5	0	1	1	0	0	0
4/24/98	DET	5	2	2	0	0	0	0
4/25/98	DET	4	0	1	0	0	0	0
4/27/98	TOR	4	0	1	0	0	0	0
4/28/98	TOR	4	0	1	0	0	0	0
4/29/98	SEA	5	2	3	1	0	1	1
4/30/98	SEA	4	1	1	0	0	0	0
5/01/98	@KC	4	0	0	0	0	0	0
5/02/98	@KC	5	2	2	0	0	1	1

Derek's major-league career batting average is .308. (AP/Wide World Photos)

Date	Opp	AB	R	H	2B	3B	HR	RBI
5/03/98	@KC	4	0	1	0	0	0	2
5/05/98	@Tex	5	1	3	0	0	0	1
5/06/98	@Tex	6	2	4	0	1	1	5
5/08/98	@Min	4	1	1	0	0	0	1
5/09/98	@Min	3	0	1	0	0	0	0
5/10/98	@Min	5	1	3	0	1	0	0
5/12/98	KC	3	1	1	0	0	0	0
5/13/98	TEX	4	2	2	0	0	1	3
5/14/98	TEX	6	0	2	0	0	0	0
5/15/98	MIN	5	1	2	0	0	1	2
5/16/98	MIN	5	3	4	1	0	0	2
5/17/98	MIN	3	0	1	0	0	0	0
5/19/98	BAL	5	0	1	0	0	0	0
5/20/98	BAL	5	2	3	1	1	0	2
5/21/98	BAL	3	0	0	0	0	0	0

Date	Opp	AB	R	H	2B	3B	HR	RBI
5/22/98	@Bos	3	0	0	0	0	0	0
5/23/98	@Bos	6	2	2	1	0	0	0
5/24/98	@Bos	6	2	3	0	0	0	2
5/25/98	@ChA	4	3	3	0	1	0	1
5/26/98	@ChA	3	2	0	0	0	0	0
5/27/98	@ChA	4	2	0	0	0	0	0
5/28/98	BOS	4	1	1	0	0	0	0
5/29/98	BOS	4	0	1	0	0	0	0
5/30/98	BOS	4	0	1	0	0	0	0
5/31/98	BOS	5	1	2	0	0	0	0
6/01/98	ChA	5	0	0	0	0	0	0
6/02/98	ChA	4	1	2	0	0	1	3
6/03/98	TB	3	1	2	0	1	0	0
6/19/98	@Cle	3	0	0	0	0	0	1
6/20/98	@Cle	5	0	1	1	0	0	0

Date	Opp	AB	R	H	2B	3B	HR	RBI
6/21/98	@Cle	3	0	1	0	0	0	0
6/22/98	ATL	5	1	1	0	0	0	0
6/23/98	ATL	4	1	1	0	0	1	1
6/24/98	@Atl	5	0	1	0	0	0	1
6/25/98	@Atl	3	1	0	0	0	0	0
6/26/98	@NYN	5	1	2	0	0	0	1
6/27/98	@NYN	5	0	1	0	0	0	2
6/28/98	@NYN	4	0	1	0	0	0	0
6/30/98	PHI	4	1	1	0	0	0	1
7/01/98	PHI	4	0	0	0	0	0	0
7/02/98	PHI	6	2	3	1	0	1	1
7/03/98	BAL	4	1	2	1	0	0	0
7/04/98	BAL	3	1	2	0	0	0	1
7/05/98	BAL	3	0	1	0	0	0	0
7/09/98	@TB	4	0	0	0	0	0	0

Date	Opp	AB	R	H	2B	3B	HR	RBI
7/10/98	@TB	5	0	1	0	0	0	0
7/11/98	@TB	4	0	0	0	0	0	0
7/12/98	@TB	5	1	2	0	0	0	2
7/13/98	@Cle	4	0	2	0	0	0	0
7/14/98	@Cle	5	1	2	0	1	0	0
7/15/98	@Det	5	0	0	0	0	0	0
7/16/98	@Det	4	0	1	0	0	0	0
7/17/98	@Tor	4	3	4	2	0	0	0
7/18/98	@Tor	6	2	2	1	0	0	0
7/19/98	@Tor	4	0	1	0	0	0	0
7/20/98	DET	8	2	4	0	0	0	0
7/20/98	DET	4	0	2	0	0	0	1
7/21/98	DET	3	2	2	0	0	1	1
7/22/98	DET	4	2	1	0	0	0	0
7/24/98	ChA	3	0	0	0	0	0	0

Date	Opp	AB	R	H	2B	3B	HR	RBI
7/25/98	ChA	5	0	2	0	0	0	1
7/26/98	ChA	4	0	0	0	0	0	0
7/28/98	@Ana	5	2	2	0	0	1	2
7/29/98	@Ana	4	2	2	0	0	1	1
7/30/98	@Ana	4	1	1	0	0	0	0
7/31/98	@Sea	5	0	1	0	0	0	0
8/01/98	@Sea	4	1	2	0	0	1	1
8/02/98	@Sea	4	0	1	0	0	0	0
8/03/98	@Oak	3	1	2	1	0	0	1
8/04/98	@Oak	3	2	2	0	0	0	0
8/04/98	@Oak	5	0	1	0	0	0	2
8/05/98	@Oak	4	0	1	1	0	0	0
8/07/98	KC	3	2	1	1	0	0	0
8/07/98	KC	5	1	0	0	0	0	0
8/08/98	KC	5	1	2	0	0	0	1

Date	Opp	AB	R	H	2B	3B	HR	RBI
8/09/98	KC	3	2	1	0	0	0	0
8/10/98	MIN	4	0	2	1	0	0	1
8/11/98	MIN	4	2	3	1	0	0	1
8/12/98	MIN	5	0	1	0	0	0	0
8/13/98	TEX	3	0	0	0	0	0	1
8/14/98	TEX	4	0	2	0	0	0	2
8/15/98	TEX	4	0	2	0	0	0	0
8/16/98	TEX	5	2	3	1	0	1	2
8/17/98	@KC	3	1	0	0	0	0	0
8/18/98	@KC	4	0	1	0	0	0	0
8/19/98	@Min	4	0	0	0	0	0	0
8/20/98	@Min	5	1	1	0	0	0	0
8/21/98	@Tex	4	1	2	0	0	1	2
8/22/98	@Tex	5	3	3	0	0	0	2
8/23/98	@Tex	5	2	3	1	0	0	1

Date	Opp	AB	R	H	2B	3B	HR	RBI
8/24/98	ANA	3	0	0	0	0	0	0
8/25/98	ANA	6	1	4	0	0	0	0
8/26/98	ANA	5	0	1	0	0	0	1
8/26/98	ANA	5	1	2	1	0	0	1
8/27/98	ANA	3	1	2	0	0	0	0
8/28/98	SEA	3	1	1	1	0	0	0
8/29/98	SEA	5	4	3	0	0	1	2
8/30/98	SEA	3	0	1	0	0	0	1
9/01/98	OAK	4	1	1	0	0	0	0
9/02/98	OAK	4	0	2	0	0	0	0
9/04/98	@ChA	5	2	2	0	0	0	1
9/05/98	@ChA	3	1	1	0	0	0	0
9/06/98	@ChA	1	0	0	0	0	0	0
9/07/98	@Bos	4	1	1	0	0	0	1
9/08/98	@Bos	2	1	0	0	0	0	0

Date	Opp	AB	R	H	2B	3B	HR	RBI
9/09/98	@Bos	4	2	2	0	0	2	2
9/10/98	TOR	5	0	0	0	0	0	0
9/11/98	TOR	4	0	0	0	0	0	0
9/12/98	TOR	4	1	1	0	0	0	0
9/13/98	TOR	3	1	1	0	1	0	2
9/14/98	BOS	4	0	0	0	0	0	0
9/15/98	BOS	4	0	1	0	0	0	0
9/16/98	@TB	4	0	1	0	0	0	0
9/17/98	@TB	5	0	1	0	0	0	0
9/18/98	@Bal	5	2	1	0	0	0	1
9/19/98	@Bal	4	0	2	0	0	0	0
9/20/98	@Bal	4	0	3	0	1	0	2
9/21/98	CLE	3	0	2	0	0	0	0
9/22/98	CLE	3	1	0	0	0	0	0
9/23/98	CLE	4	0	0	0	0	0	1

Date	Opp	AB	R	H	2B	3B	HR	RBI
9/24/98	TB	4	1	1	0	0	0	0
9/25/98	TB	4	2	2	1	0	0	0
9/26/98	TB	4	0	1	1	0	0	1
9/27/98	TB	4	1	1	0	0	0	0
Totals		**626**	**127**	**203**	**25**	**8**	**19**	**84**

1998 AL Batting Average Leaders

Bernie Williams	.339
Mo Vaughn	.337
Albert Belle	.328
Eric Davis	.327
Derek Jeter	**.324**

1998 AL Hits Leaders

Alex Rodriguez	213
Mo Vaughn	205
Derek Jeter	**203**
Albert Belle	200
Nomar Garciaparra	195

1998 AL Runs Leaders

Derek Jeter	**127**
Ray Durham	126
Alex Rodriguez	123
Ken Griffey Jr.	120
Chuck Knoblauch	117

1998 AL Stolen Base Leaders

Rickey Henderson	66
Kenny Lofton	54
Shannon Stewart	51
Alex Rodriguez	46
Jose Offerman	45
Brian Hunter	42
Tom Goodwin	38
Otis Nixon	37
Omar Vizquel	37
Ray Durham	36
Derek Jeter	**30**

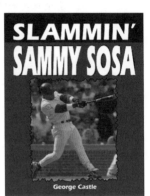

Sammy Sosa: Slammin' Sammy

Author: George Castle
ISBN: 1-58261-029-0

1998 was a break-out year for Sammy as he amassed 66 home runs, led the Chicago Cubs into the playoffs and finished the year with baseball's ultimate individual honor, MVP.

When the national spotlight was shone on Sammy during his home run chase with Mark McGwire, America got to see what a special person he is. His infectious good humor and kind heart have made him a role model across the country.

Bernie Williams: Quiet Superstar

Author: Kevin Kernan
ISBN: 1-58261-044-4

Bernie Williams, a guitar-strumming native of Puerto Rico, is not only popular with his teammates, but is considered by top team officials to be the heir to DiMaggio and Mantle fame.

He draws frequent comparisons to Roberto Clemente, perhaps the greatest player ever from Puerto Rico. Like Clemente, Williams is humble, unassuming, and carries himself with quiet dignity. Also like Clemente, he plays with rare determination and a special elegance. He's married, and serves as a role model not only for his three children, but for his young fans here and in Puerto Rico.

Sandy and Roberto Alomar:
Baseball Brothers

Author: Barry Bloom
ISBN: 1-58261-054-1

Sandy and Roberto Alomar are not just famous baseball brothers they are also famous baseball sons. Sandy Alomar, Sr. played in the major leagues fourteen seasons and later went into management. His two baseball sons have made names for themselves and have appeared in multiple All-Star games.

With Roberto joining Sandy in Cleveland, the Indians look to be a front-running contender in the American League Central.

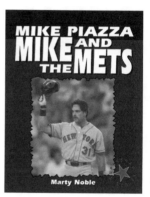

Mike Piazza:
Mike and the Mets

Author: Marty Noble
ISBN: 1-58261-051-7

A total of 1,389 players were selected ahead of Mike Piazza in the 1988 draft, who wasn't picked until the 62nd round, and then only because Tommy Lasorda urged the Dodgers to take him as a favor to his friend Vince Piazza, Mike's father.

Named in the same breath with great catchers of another era like Bench, Dickey and Berra, Mike has proved the validity of his father's constant reminder "If you work hard, dreams do come true."

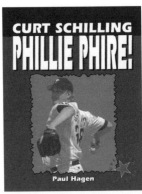

Paul Hagen

Curt Schilling: Phillie Phire!

Author: Paul Hagen
ISBN: 1-58261-055-x

Born in Anchorage, Alaska, Schilling has found a warm reception from the Philadelphia Phillies faithful. He has amassed 300+ strikeouts in the past two seasons and even holds the National League record for most strikeouts by a right handed pitcher at 319.

This book tells of the difficulties Curt faced being traded several times as a young player, and how he has been able to deal with off-the-field problems.

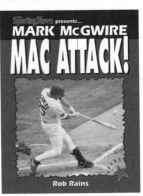

Rob Rains

Mark McGwire: Mac Attack!

Author: Rob Rains
ISBN: 1-58261-004-5

Mac Attack! describes how McGwire overcame poor eyesight and various injuries to become one of the most revered hitters in baseball today. He quickly has become a legendary figure in St. Louis, the home to baseball legends such as Stan Musial, Lou Brock, Bob Gibson, Red Schoendienst and Ozzie Smith. McGwire thought about being a police officer growing up, but he hit a home run in his first Little League at-bat and the rest is history.

Roger Clemens: Rocket Man!

Author: Kevin Kernan
ISBN: 1-58261-128-9

Alex Rodriguez: A-plus Shortstop

ISBN: 1-58261-104-1

Baseball
SuperStar Series Titles

Collect Them All!

____ **Sandy and Roberto Alomar: Baseball Brothers**

____ **Kevin Brown: Kevin with a "K"**

____ **Roger Clemens: Rocket Man!**

____ **Juan Gonzalez: Juan Gone!**

____ **Mark Grace: Winning With Grace**

____ **Ken Griffey, Jr.: The Home Run Kid**

____ **Tony Gwynn: Mr. Padre**

____ **Derek Jeter: The Yankee Kid**

____ **Randy Johnson: Arizona Heat!**

____ **Pedro Martinez: Throwing Strikes**

____ **Mike Piazza: Mike and the Mets**

____ **Alex Rodriguez: A-plus Shortstop**

____ **Curt Schilling: Philly Phire!**

____ **Sammy Sosa: Slammin' Sammy**

____ **Mo Vaughn: Angel on a Mission**

____ **Omar Vizquel: The Man with a Golden Glove**

____ **Larry Walker: Colorado Hit Man!**

____ **Bernie Williams: Quiet Superstar**

____ **Mark McGwire: Mac Attack!**

Available by calling 877-424-BOOK